The PRAYER PRINCIPLES

— for —

ENTREPRENEURS

Prayers, Strategies, and Solutions by
Entrepreneurs for Entrepreneurs

COMPILED BY

WATERSPRINGS PUBLISHING

The Prayer Principles for Entrepreneurs: Prayers, Strategies and Solutions by Entrepreneurs for Entrepreneurs

Written by Tasha Baron Smith, Brenda Burton, Shakeima Clark Chatman, Chrystal Castillo, Dr. Angela Crutchfield, Anika Davis, Kaysian Gordon, Dr. Patrice May, Stephanie Montgomery, Stacy Y. Thomas, LeWinfred Shack, Athena C. Shack, Latoyia Byrd-Williams, and Joy Yancy.

Compiled and published by Watersprings Publishing,
a division of Watersprings Media House, LLC.
P.O. Box 1284 Olive Branch, MS 38654
www.waterspringspublishing.com

Contact the publisher for bulk orders and permission requests.

Printed in the United States of America.

ISBN-13: 978-1-964972-09-1

CONTENTS

INTRODUCTION

Entrepreneurs, let's keep it real. The last few years have tested our grit, determination, and faith like never before. COVID-19 stormed in uninvited, flipping our lives and businesses upside down. It brought fears, sickness, and unimaginable loss, leaving small businesses and entrepreneurs scrambling for answers. If it wasn't cash flow issues, it was shipping delays. If it wasn't sales, it was the endless uncertainty about what tomorrow would bring. But here's the thing about Kingdom Entrepreneurs—we don't quit.

We pivoted, adjusted, and prayed harder than ever. Through it all, one thing became crystal clear: we can't do this alone. No matter how sharp our strategies or how solid our plans are, success in this marketplace requires something deeper—a connection to the ultimate CEO. That's why "The Prayer Principles for Entrepreneurs" was written.

This book is not just another "how-to" manual or business guide. It's a spiritual toolkit crafted by Kingdom Entrepreneurs who've walked through the fire and come out stronger. It's packed with prayers, solutions, and strategies designed to help you navigate the highs and lows of business life. From dealing with financial strain to finding clarity in decision-making, these pages provide you with the power of prayer combined with actionable insights.

HOW TO USE THIS BOOK

Each chapter addresses a fundamental challenge entrepreneurs face. You'll find:

- Prayers to ground you in faith and realign your focus.

- Solutions to help you tackle the issues head-on.

- Strategies to build momentum and make progress.

- Kingdom Entrepreneur tips to inspire you daily.

This book can be used as a daily devotional, a midweek reset, or a go-to resource when you're feeling stuck or uninspired. Each section is written by entrepreneurs who understand the struggle—and, more importantly, the breakthroughs.

And here's the best part: the authors of this book are here to connect with you. Flip to the back for their bios, contact information, and ways to reach out. Whether it's a prayer request, a business question, or a word of encouragement, we're in this together.

So, grab your coffee (or tea), get comfy, and let this book remind you that you're not alone in this journey. Together, we'll turn those setbacks into setups for your next level. Ready to unlock those blessings? Let's get to it.

1

WISDOM FIRST

"Wisdom is the principal thing; Therefore, get wisdom. And in all your getting, get understanding." Proverbs 4:5, NKJV

Time is a commodity that cannot be replaced or reproduced. Once it is gone, it is gone. We are all gifted with the same 24 hours in a day. The question is, are we using our time effectively? As entrepreneurs, we need to balance our time between work, play, and rest in order to be successful. Authorpreneurs are not exempt from this balancing act, and many of us believe that our greatest success is primarily based on inspiration, that unless we are inspired, we will experience writer's block, and our creative juices will not flow. Uninspired seasons when you are not in a place to fulfill your obligations without a struggle are unavoidable but, as an entrepreneur - author or otherwise - you are still required to press toward productivity until your assignment is complete. Pressing when you don't feel like pressing requires discipline. Discipline, according to an online definition based on data from Oxford Languages, is the ability to "train oneself to do something in a controlled and habitual way." Discipline may be hard, but it is necessary to fulfill our entrepreneurial obligations (in my case, finishing, marketing, or selling books) within our chosen fields.

Without a doubt, discipline is a significant requirement for a successful entrepreneur, but one other prayer principle is even more important: wisdom. Wisdom guides you to be consistent and disciplined. As a pastor, authorpreneur, wife and caregiver, I apply wisdom so that I use my time well. My seven years of experience as a pastor and serving as an associate minister for seven years prior has proven that wisdom is the principal thing.

One online definition of wisdom based on data from Oxford Languages states that wisdom is "the quality of having experience, knowledge, and good judgment; the quality of being wise", and the Bible further expounds that wisdom comes from God (Proverbs 2:6 NKJV). Proverbs 4:7 (NKJV) states, *"Wisdom is the principal thing... get wisdom. Get understanding."* To be the best entrepreneur you can be requires wisdom. Pastoring a church is equivalent to operating a non-profit business. Self-publishing books is similar to operating a for-profit business. To succeed in both arenas, I lean on the wisdom of the Word. Since wisdom is the principal (primary, most important) thing, I encourage you to exercise wisdom first in all that you do. I hope you will seriously consider utilizing the following three pairs of wisdom principles so that you may obtain understanding and achieve success: prayer and praise, preparation and prioritization, and productivity and performance.

1. Prayer and Praise

Begin and end each day with prayer. Pray for direction when you wake up. Pray for peaceful rest when go to sleep. Ask God for discernment and guidance as you begin your day so that you use your time well. Pray throughout the day so you don't miss God speaking adjustments to your schedule. Praise God for opportunities when you wake-up and show gratitude for accomplishments made during the day before going to bed. I have a gratitude journal on my nightstand, and each night before bed, I list at least three things for which I am grateful. I also list things I want to do better the next day based on what I learned today. Let the last thing you do before bed reflect your gratitude for the day. Praise God for all that He has done. It is also wise to go to sleep on the Word. Positive thoughts lead to peaceful sleep (Psalm 4:8, NKJV), and peaceful sleep aids in attaining the next wisdom principle pair, preparation, and prioritization.

2. Preparation and Prioritization

Prepare and prioritize *each* day with God's guidance. Matthew 6:34 (NKJV) reminds us not to worry about tomorrow, for tomorrow will worry about its own things. While we all have long-term goals and plans for various lengths of time, wisdom dictates that we ask for direction each day to make the best of our 24 hours. As an author, pastor, wife, long-distance caregiver to aging parents, and individual contributor at a major corporation, among other roles, I cannot trust how I spend my day to chance, and neither should you. While there should be room for flexibility, I recommend a general plan or schedule for the week. List three to five things you plan to accomplish daily based on that schedule. Notate how much time you will spend on those tasks and when you will complete them. Make schedules based on categories, if necessary. For example, in extremely busy seasons, I have a to-do list for writing assignments and a to-do list for church business.

> **Kingdom Entrepreneur Tip**
>
> Put first things first! Prioritize and practice wisdom daily.
>
> *—Joy Yancy*

Allow God to direct your daily schedule (Isaiah 30:21), including a time for sleep, particularly if you have trouble shutting down at night. The last item on your to-do list for each day should be a wind down to rest and sleep. Intentionality may be required if you find yourself running on fumes at the end of every day. Schedule rest and relaxation for both the short-term and long-term. Rest restores and enables you to do more. Preparing and prioritizing properly leads to the third wisdom principle pair: productivity and performance.

3. Productivity and Performance

Making a to-do list and completing it are not the same. Completing a task requires the act of walking in wisdom. It reinforces that responsibility must come before fun. Procrastination must take a back seat. In the words of Nike, "Just Do It." You must provide a quality product or service that satisfies your customer. As an author and digital creator, my audience of readers and social media followers have an expectation. They look for an encouraging word to start their day and bring them joy. I must produce original content consistently and with excellence. I am committed to showing up consistently at 6:33 a.m. CST on Facebook and Instagram M-F with a "Morning Joy" post to add positivity to their day. As a pastor, I am expected to preach a sermon every Sunday with power and good news. What are you producing? Are you meeting the expectations of your customers? Are you producing and performing for God's glory and other's good? It is wise to seek God's approval (Galatians 1:10) so that you may experience success.

PRAYER FOR WISDOM

Gracious God,

Wisdom comes from You, and the Word says wisdom is the principal thing. As I begin my day, I seek Your wisdom and guidance. Before I get out of bed, I pursue Your knowledge. James 1:5 (NKJV) says, *"If any of you lacks wisdom, let him ask of God, who gives to all liberally and without reproach, and it will be given to him."* I come today as humbly as I know how to ask for wisdom to operate my business. I ask for understanding to effectively balance running my business with maintaining my relationships (my relationship with my spouse, with my children, with my parents, with my friends, and with my employees).

I strive to begin and end each day with prayer and praise, to gain clarity on how to prepare and prioritize my day in order to maximize productivity and achieve optimal performance for Your glory and my good. Allow Your wisdom to work through me to inspire, edify, and encourage every customer (client, congregant, reader, etc.) in my sphere of influence. As I daily follow these ***wisdom principle pairs*** of prayer and praise, preparation and prioritization, and productivity and performance, may goodness and mercy follow me. As I make the main thing the main thing, I trust that You, Lord, will make my way prosperous and give me good success (Joshua 1:8, NKJV). In Jesus name, Amen!

-Joy W. Yancy,

Pastor and Authorpreneur

Seek God's Vision First

Pray for clarity on God's purpose for your business, aligning your goals with His will.

"Commit to the Lord whatever you do, and he will establish your plans."

– Proverbs 16:3

$$2$$

PREPARE YOUR S.O.I.L. FOR GROWTH

"Let us not become weary in doing good, for at the proper time we will reap a harvest if we do not give up." Galatians 6:9

As entrepreneurs, our journeys are often marked by moments of triumph and seasons of trial. While we may have started with high hopes and clear visions, the path to success can be loaded with challenges that test our faith, resilience, and resolve. My own journey began in 2011, during what was known as the worst housing crisis in history. It was a time when success seemed impossible, and I was often left wondering if I had made the right decision to quit my job and follow what I believed was a calling from God to start my real estate business.

For nine months, I worked tirelessly without a single sale. I was pregnant with real estate, so to speak—working hard, planting seeds, but seeing no growth. Instead of a flood of clients, I was met with frustration, doubt, and an ever-growing stack of bills. I began questioning my calling and felt the weight of discouragement pressing down on me. But through these trials, I learned a valuable lesson: in order to thrive, I had to prepare my S.O.I.L. for growth.

S - Surrender to Something Bigger Than Yourself

"Commit your actions to the Lord, and your plans will succeed."
— Proverbs 16:3 (NLT)

When I started, I thought my success depended entirely on me. I worked hard but lacked direction. It wasn't until I surrendered my business to God that I began to see progress. Surrendering doesn't mean giving up; it means acknowledging that you are part of something bigger and seeking God's guidance for your steps. I learned that God doesn't compete with the noise in our lives. Only when I quieted myself and made time for prayer and meditation did I begin receiving divine guidance. This led to new marketing strategies, content ideas, and even clarity on financial decisions. I started praying intentionally, asking God to guide me to the right clients and open the right doors. Soon, clients began saying, "I prayed about who to hire as a real estate agent, and God led me to you." That's the power of surrender!

If you're struggling in your business, I encourage you to spend intentional time in prayer. Just as you'd take a car to its manufacturer when it breaks down, take your business to its Creator when you need direction.

O - Oust Bad Habits

"Do not be conformed to this world, but be transformed by the renewal of your mind." – Romans 12:2 (ESV)

Once I surrendered, I realized that no matter how hard I worked, toxic habits were holding me back. I lacked structure, was reactive instead of proactive, and often entertained negative thoughts. One of the first things I did was establish a routine through time blocking, allocating specific times for prospecting, client meetings, marketing, and administrative tasks. This added structure to my day and increased my productivity. I also became mindful of my words, realizing that what I spoke often shaped my reality. I stopped saying, "This market is tough," and started speaking positivity over my business. Finally, I distanced myself from negative conversations and social media influences that drained my energy. By ousting these bad habits, I made room for growth.

I - Invest in Your Biggest Asset (You)

"The heart of the discerning acquires knowledge, for the ears of the wise seek it out." – Proverbs 18:15 (NIV)

One of the most important lessons I learned was that I am my business's most valuable asset. My personal growth directly influenced my business success. Jim Rohn said, "Your level of success will seldom exceed your level of personal development." I began investing in myself by attending conferences, hiring coaches, and seeking mentorship. One pivotal moment was attending the Act Like a Success conference hosted by Steve Harvey, which reignited my passion and gave me actionable strategies for my business. In addition to attending events, I made learning a part of my daily routine. I listened to audio books and podcasts during my commute and dedicated time to read each month. I also prioritized my physical and mental health, ensuring I had the energy and clarity needed to run my business effectively. When you invest in yourself, you're not just growing your skills but also expanding your capacity. The more you grow, the more your business will grow.

L - Leverage Your Relationships

"Two people are better off than one, for they can help each other succeed." – Proverbs 27:17 (NIV)

No one succeeds alone. I currently lead a real estate team, coach new agents in my brokerage, host an annual conference for teen girls through a nonprofit, serve on a couple of nonprofit boards, and I am a leader in a few organizations. I could never do it all without leveraging the relationships I've built over the years. Initially, I believed the myth that I had to do everything myself. But as I started delegating tasks and trusting others, my business flourished. Building a strong team was essential. I hired people who were strong in areas where I was weak, which freed me to focus on my strengths and grow the business.

Leveraging relationships doesn't stop at your team. Your personal network of friends and family can also be a valuable resource. Don't hesitate to ask for help, whether it's watching the kids for an afternoon or providing input on a new idea. As you grow your business, make sure to continue expanding your professional network by attending events and joining organizations.

Leverage also goes both ways—be willing to offer support and guidance to others. When you build relationships based on mutual benefit, you create a network that will lift you up during challenges and celebrate with you during successes.

The Harvest

You're ready to plant the seeds of success once you've prepared your S.O.I.L. by surrendering, ousting bad habits, investing in yourself, and leveraging relationships. But growth doesn't happen overnight. Like a farmer tending crops, you must nurture your business with patience and persistence.

The seeds you plant today may take time to bear fruit, but when they do, the harvest will be abundant. This harvest won't just be a testament to your hard work but to the principles that have guided you along the way—your faith, perseverance, and commitment to personal and professional growth. The work doesn't stop when success comes. Just as a farmer continues to care for the soil after a harvest, you must keep nurturing your business foundation. Continue learning, growing, and evolving to ensure your success is sustainable.

Conclusion

Preparing your S.O.I.L. for growth is an ongoing process. Surrender to something bigger than yourself, oust bad habits, invest in your personal and professional development, and leverage the relationships around you. When you follow these principles, you create an environment where your business can thrive.

Remember, success is not a destination—it's a journey. Stay committed to these principles, and trust that the seeds you plant will grow into a harvest of success, purpose, and fulfillment. And don't forget to enjoy the journey along the way!

PRAYER FOR GROWTH

Heavenly Father,

Thank You for the vision and opportunities You have placed before me. I surrender my business to You, trusting that You will guide my steps and lead me toward success. Grant me the wisdom to oust bad habits that hinder my growth and the discipline to establish routines that honor You.

Lord, help me invest in myself, seek knowledge, and grow both personally and professionally. Grant me divine connections and relationships that uplift and support me and help me leverage these connections for Your glory. As I prepare my S.O.I.L. for growth, I trust that You will bring forth an abundant and overflowing harvest. In Jesus' name, I pray, Amen.

- Shakeima Clark Chatman,
Real Estate Agent, Coach and Author of
Possess the Land: The Believer's Guide to
Homebuying

3

WISDOM FROM WORMS AND BIRDS

"So I tell you, don't worry about the things you need to live—what you will eat, drink, or wear. Life is more important than food, and the body is more important than what you put on it. Look at the birds. They don't plant, harvest, or save food in barns, but your heavenly Father feeds them. Don't you know you are worth much more than they are?"
- Matthew 6: 25-26 (ERV)

'Cause every little thing is gonna be all right!"
- Bob Marley's, Three Little Birds

On mornings when I sit on my patio to have coffee and devotion time, I have the privilege of not only having the sun shine directly on me (unless it's a cloudy day) but also the privilege of seeing and hearing the birds as they sing, chirp and go about their day. Oftentimes, no matter what passage of scripture I might be reading and studying, the sounds of the birds will arrest my attention and the lyrics to a Bob Marley's song above will come to mind. It is at that moment I have to stop what I'm currently reading and just thank God that *everything is going to be alright*. I don't have to worry about a thing because God got me!

As Kingdom Entrepreneurs, we can sometimes (or a lot of times) find ourselves worrying about all the things we need to live and sustain our lives and families. You know about those worries don't you? We have to have enough money and resources to maintain our homes,

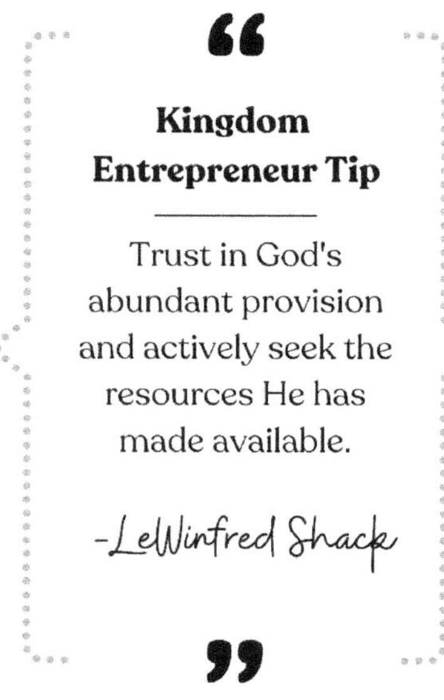

maintain and grow our businesses, make payroll if we have employees, and find money and resources to invest in ourselves. I don't think I'm by myself when I say that there are times when there is more month than money; it can be very disheartening, disappointing, and discouraging to your entrepreneurial spirit. You know what God has promised, but it sometimes seems like the math just ain't mathing. In these times, we have to remember, trust in, and lean on the promises of God. You have to reflect on what God has said as it pertains to you. And when the anxiety kicks in, and your heart and mind are racked with worry, hear the song of the birds as they croon to you: *"Don't worry, 'cause every little thing is going to be alright!"* Hear the voice of God as he reminds you that if he takes care of the birds, surely he will take care of you.

I did not truly understand my infatuation with the birds until one day, after praying about this scripture, I went for a walk through my neighborhood. As I walked down the blocks and walked through the park, I noticed that there was an abundance of worms all over the sidewalks. Whether they were small and skinny, or big and juicy, there was an abundance of them everywhere. I also noticed that no matter how many birds swooped down and ate them, there was still an abundance left over. So many that some of them had actually dried up died because they had not been eaten, and could not get back to the refuge of the grass and soil before the heat caused them to dry out.

God began to speak to me at the sight of all these worms. He showed me that we are the birds, and the worms are his provision. He knows what we need, and because we are His, He provides for us in abundance. There were so many worms available—to the point that many had dried up and died—because the birds had not taken advantage of all that was made available to them.

As Kingdom Entrepreneurs and children of God, we have to have the faith to believe that God has and will provide everything we need to live in abundance as entrepreneurs. Then we must put this faith to work by actively seeking out the wisdom and resources available to us as business owners. And remember this: God's Word trumps the old adage "that the early bird gets the worm." No, no, no! The bird that gets the worm is the one who swoops in and takes advantage of all that is made available to them. So, even if your worries and fears have led to complacency and procrastination, receive the grace and mercy of God, and go get your worms!

PRAYER FOR PROVISION

Heavenly Father,

Thank You for Your loving care and provision in my life. As I reflect on Your words, I'm reminded of Your unfailing faithfulness. Just as You provide for the birds of the air, I trust that You will meet all my needs.

Lord, forgive me for the times I've allowed my worries to distract me from Your will and Your promises for my life. Help me to seek Your kingdom first, knowing that You are aware of everything I need. Strengthen my faith to rely on Your providence rather than my own efforts.

Father, thank You for valuing me more than the birds, which You so beautifully created and care for. When worry and anxiety creeps in, remind me of Your constant presence and sustaining power in my life. Help me to trust in Your creative provision, even when it comes in unexpected ways.

Ignite me with Divine focus, strategy, and energy to create the life and business You have promised me. May I seek Your face, Your will, and Your kingdom above all else. Thank You for Your promise to provide all I need as I pursue righteousness.

In Jesus' name, I pray. Amen.

-LeWinfred A. Shack,
*Author of Overcoming Anxiety
and Licensed Massage Therapist*

4

CHECK YOUR CIRCLE

"As iron sharpens, so one person sharpens another."
Proverbs 27:17, NIV

As an entrepreneur and author, I quickly learned how important and vital it is to listen and learn from those who have been in the business longer than I have. Being open to advice and wisdom from those around me has been a tremendous blessing, and it still is. For example, I remember vending at an event and being surrounded by dynamic business owners. While chatting with a seasoned entrepreneur, she shared valuable pointers and ideas with me, such as marketing strategies and examples of items to purchase to promote my brand through signage and table displays.

Additionally, she suggested revising my business cards and other business platforms. Although brief, the time spent with this individual was full of knowledge, inspiration, and encouragement that challenged me to expand and sharpen my thinking on the limitless possibilities for my business and the significance of building my brand. The information received was so helpful for me, that as soon as I completed that event, I updated my business cards to include QR codes directing people to the website, and I ordered a customized table runner with my brand information for display when vending. These words of wisdom not only helped me do things to promote the business, but they also gave me inspiration and ideas that I had not considered on my own.

This entrepreneurial journey takes persistent effort and action. Businesses remind me of plants: if you care for them, they grow; if you neglect them, they fizzle out. That's why it's critical to know that becoming an entrepreneur requires time, patience, diligence, and commitment to navigate the ups and downs. Therefore, surround yourself with people

who genuinely help and support your growth.

It is crucial to approach these connections with wisdom and discernment to ensure that you are connected to the right individuals who can positively impact your life. The Bible verse Proverbs 27:17 succinctly conveys the importance of surrounding yourself with the right people. The book of Proverbs is a rich source of wisdom that provides practical insights on navigating life's challenges. It draws on the accumulated knowledge and experiences of the elders, particularly focusing on the wisdom attributed to King Solomon.

The wisdom found in the book of Proverbs involves the careful application of Biblical truths to daily life. When one integrates God's principles into practical decision-making, it leads to a life characterized by wisdom and righteousness. This means that seeking wise counsel and associating with individuals who exemplify wisdom is an essential aspect of personal growth and moral development.

Proverbs 27:17 serves as a powerful reminder of the impact of our connections in shaping our thoughts and influencing our decisions. The people we choose to associate with and the environments we immerse ourselves in play a pivotal role in broadening our perspectives. Therefore, it is vital to be intentional about surrounding ourselves with individuals who challenge and refine our thinking, provide support in decision-making processes, and contribute to the enrichment of our spiritual lives.

It is important to remember in entrepreneurship, there is no one-size-fits-all approach because our businesses, like ourselves, are unique. Our company strategy, services, products, and organizational structures vary. All business entrepreneurs, however, recognize the importance of surrounding themselves with the appropriate people. As an entrepreneur, stay open to new learning opportunities and engage and network with others who reflect where you want to see your company go. Networking is not just about making connections; it's about opening doors to new opportunities and collaborations. Embrace your fundamental values and beliefs and seek support and encouragement as you continue to grow and expand your business. Give yourself grace in the process, knowing that this is a continual learning and development process. Furthermore, connect with others who will pray for and with you and encourage you and your aspirations. Finally, get in the room of entrepreneurs and business owners to sharpen who you are as a person and a business owner.

PRAYER FOR YOUR CIRCLE

Most gracious, loving, and wise God, Lord, thank you for the wisdom of Your word. I pray that You would help me embrace Your wisdom and hide it in my heart so I can live according to Your will and way daily. God, it is my prayer that as I continue to grow in wisdom, You would please remove anything or anyone that does not bring value to my life and that You would surround me with the right people who will encourage and inspire me to be the best version of myself that I have been called to be.

God, I pray that as I strive to live a life of wisdom in You, I will apply Your instructions and precepts in my personal and professional life. Your guidance is paramount in every decision I make as an entrepreneur, and I trust in Your wisdom. Please allow my business to be a blessing to all it serves, and as I grow and develop, surround me with those who will sharpen me, push me, and inspire me while allowing me space to grow and evolve into the change maker You have called me to be. I thank God in advance for a circle that continuously sharpens me along this journey so that I can, in turn, inspire and empower another entrepreneur along the way. In Jesus Name, I pray, Amen.

-Anika Davis,
Coach, Consultant, and Author of
Meditations of a Mother's Heart

5

IT'S TIME TO FACE YOUR FEARS

"Have I not commanded you? Be strong and of good courage; do not be afraid, nor be dismayed, for the Lord your God is with you wherever you go."
Joshua 1:9, NKJV

It's been said that "we cannot change what we refuse to confront." This statement is a bittersweet truth because we tend to like the idea or the concept of change, but we don't want to confront those barriers that are prone to prohibit our ability to grow or change. Fear is one of the most prominent barriers we are often reluctant to face. Fear is a peculiar emotion because it can function as a double-edged sword, whereas fear can appear healthy or unhealthy. Healthy fear drives our nervous system and gives us the survival skills to stay safe from danger. On the other hand, unhealthy fear places us on unnecessary alert, making us more cautious than we need to be and, therefore, preventing us from moving forward. To control those unhealthy moments of fear, we must resolve to confront them head-on.

As an entrepreneur, a significant aspect of the journey involves boldly confronting and challenging your fears. When I ventured into entrepreneurship, my mind swirled with countless thoughts and questions. Where should I start? How do I even begin? I eagerly immersed myself in master classes, diligently jotting down the wisdom of successful business leaders. Yet, I discovered that actualizing their advice was more daunting than merely absorbing it. Consequently, I set my notes aside. However, about a year later, a surge of ambition and vision sparked

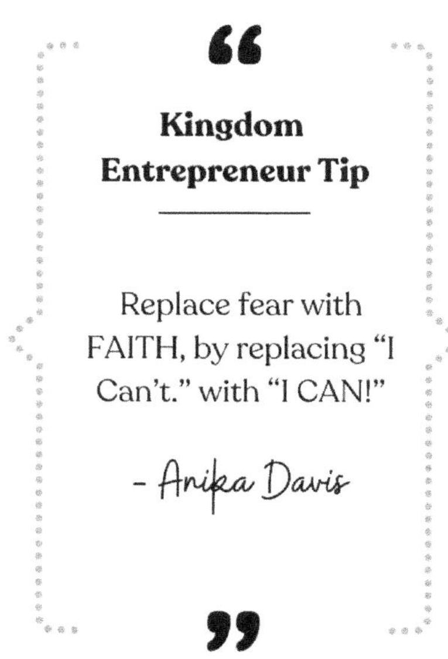

within me, forcing me to revisit those initial questions. I recognized that to bring my business to life; I had to courageously embrace my fears and take a leap of faith, even if it meant feeling scared. With each step I took, the elusive answers I sought slowly materialized. Without facing my fears, I wouldn't have been able to muster the courage to launch.

This text found in Joshua chapter 1:9 provides instructions on how to confront our fear. From the beginning of this narrative, we are immediately inserted into God's conversation with Joshua. Following the death of Moses, God gave precise instructions to Joshua to help him as he led the people of Israel into the Promised Land, which He swore He would give to their ancestors. This commissioning from God would not be easy; Joshua was a newly appointed leader of the people who had lost their long-time leader, Moses, and now he must bring them into their Promised Land while overcoming the opposition. For Joshua to successfully fulfill the work that God called him to do, to lead the Israelites into Canaan, to divide up the land among the people, and to confront any fears that may arise on the journey, Joshua was going to have to do as God commanded, be bold and courageous.

In this entrepreneurship journey, I encourage you to confront your fears consistently. This journey is not cookie-cutter. Instead, it is unique to us and the vision that God has placed within us. Sometimes, the vision can appear so grand and large that you can become overwhelmed by just the mere thought of it. But I implore you to remain obedient to God's will and keep going despite fear.

Here's the real: there will be days where you feel uncertain, there will be days where you feel unsure, there will be days where it seems like you have no idea what you are doing, there will be days where fear will try to sneak up on you and cause you to doubt and question everything that you are doing. Nevertheless, keep pushing, keep praying, and keep seeking God because it is in our constant pursuit of God's will that we will be able to confront our fears and create change knowing that God is with us. And since God is with us, we don't have to fear, but we can be bold and courageous, knowing that in God, there is no failure.

PRAYER FOR FAITH

Gracious God,

I just come before you, thanking You, O God, for being a great God, Thanking You, O God, for being a purposeful God, Thanking You, O God, for being a strategic God. Because You are a God of purpose and intention, I thank You for the plans You have intentionally proposed for my life. God, I may not always understand Your ways, I may not understand Your thoughts, or Your Plans, but I can rest assured knowing that You, O God, have a plan for my life, and because of Your plan for my life, I don't have to worry, and I don't have to fret. All I have to do is place my faith in You.

And in those moments, God, when I find myself experiencing feelings of fear, fear of failure, fear of inadequacy, or fear of uncertainty, I can be reminded of the words you spoke to Joshua, and I can move forward with boldness and courage knowing God that You are with me. And because You are with me, I can replace fear with faith. So, God, I pray that You continue to walk with me, stir up the gifts in me, and continue to lead, guide, and direct me as only You can. In Jesus' name. Amen

-Anika Davis,
Coach, Consultant, and Author of
Meditations of a Mother's Heart

6

DECLARE YOUR EXPANSION SEASON

Enlarge the place of your tent, stretch your tent curtains wide, do not hold back; lengthen your cords, strengthen your stakes. For you will spread out to the right and to the left; your descendants will dispossess nations and settle in their desolate cities.
Isaiah 54:2-3, NIV

Something miraculous happens when you decide where you are is no longer where you want to be. To create a new reality and life for yourself requires a journey of expansion. Declare this is your *expansion season*. Personal expansion is the transformative journey of stretching your capabilities, mindset, and experiences. It's about daring to venture beyond the familiar, embracing fresh challenges, and committing to lifelong learning and growth. Expansion also means releasing spaces, people, and even clients who do not align with who you are and the results you are creating.

Expansion and declaring your expansion season are significant because, as Jim Rohn stated for decades, "for things to change, you have to change, and for things to get better, you have to get better." In order to change any circumstance, we ourselves must become greater than those circumstances and most importantly, we must believe in the *possibility* of overcoming and take action aligned to bring that vision and desire to pass.

A year ago, I declared my expansion season. I was in a bad place emotionally and financially. Before that declaration, I served my husband and children as a military spouse and stay-at-home mom. Most caregivers know the sacrifices that are made in these situations. In my case, I let myself go completely. I had no personal income, my credit score plummeted, I gained over 50 pounds. One day I looked in the mirror and did not recognize myself. I declared this is my expansion season. I decided to transform and renew my mind and become the most powerful version of myself.

Within six months of declaring my expansion season, I acquired an office location for my business, L3 Virtual solutions, LLC. We are a bookkeeping and business consulting firm. Today I serve multiple clients in both categories. Not only do I have Bookkeeping clients, but I also have consulting clients, and I coach other bookkeepers through their expansion season. I didn't know it would look like this when I declared my expansion season. In fact, it looks a lot better than I imagined.

There are three main areas of expansion I'd like to highlight in this chapter:

1. Identity

2. Courage

3. Aligned Action

IDENTITY

How do you see yourself? Take a moment and journal this intentionally:

What do you believe is possible for you? Who are you? Not what you do. Who are you at your core when things are good and when things are not so good?

For example, a bookkeeper is not who I am. It's a task I do and I'm able to perform. It's a skill set. If I didn't perform bookkeeping services, I would still be me, and as an entrepreneur, be able to earn how I please. Your position at a company does not define you because who you are at your core is who you are whether you hold the specific position or not. This is how I answer the question of who I am: "I am a conductor of

God's power in this Earth. God's love, power, and creativity flow through me."

COURAGE

It takes courage to do things differently. Everyone will be taken aback by your new habits and walking in your power, and you may be concerned about being judged. You may be concerned about appearing to be proud. We all know the scripture so well that pride comes before a fall. Remember, humility is between you and God and in order for you to fulfill your purpose you have to walk in courage and confidence. Humility does not mean shrinking, playing small, or dumbing down your intellect. Be courageous and fulfill the desires God placed in your heart.

A big part of courage is also being obedient to do the little things God told you to do. We have no idea how those little things connect to the big picture or our goals, but God does. In most cases, in hindsight, we see how everything aligned. Do the little things God tells you to do, without being concerned with being judged by others or appearing silly.

ALIGNED ACTION

Now this is important because action does not mean busy. Many people are busy doing nothing and going nowhere. You want your actions to connect to the desired outcome yet still knowing you are not defined by the result. Your actions should be intentional and with purpose with your goal in mind.

One final thought. When you declare your expansion season, everything is not going to be roses, peaches and cream, rainbows and sunshine. There will be some storms and a lot of distractions yet in all these things we are more than conquerors through Christ Jesus. So, I encourage you not to let these storms thwart your expansion. Let the water from the rain help you grow and decide to flourish, even if that means flourishing in chaos. Above all, stay connected to our Heavenly Father because He is our source and always brings the increase.

Finally, keep moving forward. Cheers to your expansion journey. It's expansion season.

PRAYER PRINCIPLE

Invite God into Every Decision

Make prayer a priority before making big or small decisions, trusting His guidance over your own understanding.

"In all your ways submit to him, and he will make your paths straight."

– Proverbs 3:6

PRAYER FOR EXPANSION SEASON

Heavenly Father,

I come before You today with a heart full of gratitude. Your Word assures me that You have plans to prosper me and not to harm me, plans to give me hope and a future (Jeremiah 29:11). I stand on this promise, trusting in Your divine plan for my life. Lord, I ask for Your wisdom and guidance as I seek to expand in every area of my life. As it is written, "Enlarge the place of your tent, stretch your tent curtains wide, do not hold back; lengthen your cords, strengthen your stakes" (Isaiah 54:2). I pray that You help me to boldly step into new territories, expanding my influence and impact for Your glory.

Father, I pray for the strength and courage to embrace the opportunities You present before me. You said in Your Word, "I can do all things through Christ who strengthens me" (Philippians 4:13). Empower me with Your Spirit to overcome any challenges and to rise above any obstacles that may come my way. Lord, as I expand, I pray for an increase in wisdom, discernment, and understanding. Your Word says, "If any of you lacks wisdom, you should ask God, who gives generously to all without finding fault, and it will be given to you" (James 1:5). I seek Your wisdom, Lord, to make the right decisions and to walk in the path You have set for me. Finally, Lord, I pray that my expansion will be a testimony of Your goodness and faithfulness. May it bring glory to Your name and draw others closer to You.

In Jesus' mighty name, I pray.

-Tasha Baron Smith,
Mentor and Life-Strategist
Coach

Pray for Wisdom and Discernment

Ask God for the wisdom to make sound business decisions and discernment to recognize opportunities and challenges.

"If any of you lacks wisdom, you should ask God, who gives generously to all without finding fault, and it will be given to you."

– James 1:5

7

RELINQUISH YOUR CONTROL AND

EMBRACE GOD'S POWER

"In their hearts humans plan their course, but the Lord establishes their steps."
Proverbs 16:9 (NIV)

As entrepreneurial leaders, one of our greatest challenges is the temptation to control every aspect of our course. We often find ourselves navigating the delicate balance between ambition and anxiety, trying to orchestrate outcomes according to our limited understanding. This quest for control can lead to stress, burnout, and ultimately hinder the very growth we seek. You want to embrace the power of divine guidance and release the illusion of control. This becomes a true demonstration of our faith in God's divine power.

I've experienced firsthand the pitfalls of trying to control every detail. The more I grasped for control, the more I felt disconnected from the flow of innovation and creativity. It was a journey marked by tension and frustration until I realized that true progress requires a shift in perspective—from control to trust in the true power that only comes from faith in God.

Consideration must be given to acknowledging our limitations and recognizing that our strength is fueled by God's power. When we release the need to control every outcome and instead surrender to the leading of God's wisdom, we tap into a wellspring of inspiration, creativity, and provision beyond our own capabilities. As entrepreneurial leaders, let our quest be for God's power. To lead with God's power is to lead from a place of faith. It is a journey of continual alignment with our divine God-defined purpose, trusting in the unfolding of our destiny.

Often, we find ourselves at the crossroads of power and control, grappling with the tension between God's guidance and worldly desires. Proverbs 16:9 reminds us that while we may earnestly plan our course, it is ultimately the Lord who establishes our steps. This scripture serves as a beacon of wisdom, urging us to trust God's divine orchestration of our lives and work. When we embrace the power that comes from aligning our hearts with the will of our Maker, we position ourselves for success that transcends our limited understanding.

As entrepreneurial leaders, let us release the grip of control and embrace the transformative power of divine guidance. By surrendering our plans and ambitions to the wisdom of the Lord, we open ourselves to a path of abundance, purpose, and fulfillment beyond our wildest dreams. Let's harness the true power of God's wisdom and guidance for our entrepreneurial journey.

Proverbs 16:9 also reminds us that our efforts to control are futile in the face of the Lord's sovereignty. It is He who establishes our steps, shaping our path guided by His greater purpose and wisdom. This scripture underscores the profound truth that divine guidance is not just a comforting notion but a source of true power in our entrepreneurial endeavors.

PRAYER TO EMBRACE GOD'S POWER

Gracious God,

I come before you humbly, recognizing my need for Your divine guidance in my entrepreneurial journey. I confess the times I have relied solely on my own understanding, and I now surrender my plans and ambitions to you.

Lord, establish my steps according to your perfect will. Open my eyes to see the opportunities you have prepared for me. I acknowledge that true power comes from walking in alignment with your purpose. Help me to trust in your timing and provision, even when circumstances seem uncertain. May Your wisdom guide my decisions, and Your favor surround me like a shield.

Empower me, Lord, to lead with integrity and humility and not control. Let your light shine through me in every interaction and transaction. As I navigate the challenges of entrepreneurship, let me be a vessel of your grace and love.

Thank you, Father, for your unwavering presence and guidance. I surrender control to You, knowing that your plans for me are good and full of hope.

In Jesus' name, Amen.

- Dr. Angela Crutchfield,
Certified Coach and Speaker

Surrender the Outcome

Trust God with the results, whether success or failure, knowing He is working all things together for good.

"And we know that in all things God works for the good of those who love him, who have been called according to his purpose."

– Romans 8:28

SERVANT LEADERSHIP IN THE DAILY GRIND

"Do nothing out of selfish ambition or vain conceit. Rather, in humility value others above yourselves, not looking to your own interests but each of you to the interests of the others."
Philippians 2:3-4, NIV

Have you ever had a customer service experience where you walked away saying, "They clearly are having a bad day"? It's a sentiment many of us have encountered, where the demeanor of the service provider seems to reflect their internal struggles rather than the quality of service we expect. As leaders we must examine precisely this phenomenon—how our challenges as entrepreneurs and the demands of the daily grind can seep into our interactions with customers, resulting in an experience that falls short of excellence. The underlying message is clear: the customer experience should not change based on our experiences behind the scenes as business owners.

It's easy for the mundane routine to turn into a default, curt demeanor that can alienate others, negatively impact our customers and hinder our effectiveness as leaders with our clients, teams, or business partners. As entrepreneurs, our days are often filled with a flurry of activity, from managing finances to overseeing operations, dealing with suppliers, and attending to customer needs. The challenge lies in maintaining a spirit of servant leadership amidst the demands of running a business.

> **Kingdom Entrepreneur Tip**
>
> Your attitude sets the tone for your interactions—start each day with a moment of reflection on demonstrating compassionate leadership.
>
> —Dr. Angela Crutchfield

Within this hustle and bustle of daily tasks, we often easily lose sight of the human aspect of leadership and succumb to the pressures of the management of the daily grind. The challenge becomes even more pronounced when we consider the delicate balance between attending to innumerable tasks and upholding servant leadership principles. Beyond merely managing tasks, we're called upon to lead by inspiring and guiding others, fostering an environment of collaboration, trust, and respect. Yet, as the demands of the business mount, we may unintentionally slip into a mode of autopilot, where interactions with others become transactional rather than transformational. This shift can gradually erode the structure of our leadership effectiveness as our warm and engaging demeanor gives way to a mechanical, impersonal approach. The relational aspect of entrepreneurship must be preserved as it is the core of our success.

This concern expands into what can be tagged as the leadership danger zone of allowing the mundane work routine to dictate our behavior. This leadership danger zone extends beyond the all-too-common negative impact on us as leaders (stress, anger, fatigue, etc.), by expanding to other individuals around us, ultimately resulting in irreversible damaging interactions with customers. A curt demeanor born out of sheer exhaustion or being overwhelmed can inadvertently alienate those we serve, tarnishing the reputation of our business and eroding customer loyalty. In a world where positive experiences and genuine connections drive customer loyalty, the impact of such failures in service excellence cannot be overstated. Thus, the challenge for entrepreneurs becomes twofold: not only must we navigate the complexities of the day-to-day management of a business, but we must also safeguard against the gradual erosion of our capacity for compassionate leadership within the daily routine.

Philippians 2:3-4 reminds us of the importance of humility and considering others' needs ahead of our own. As leaders, our focus should extend beyond our ambitions and shortcomings to genuinely caring for the well-being, engagement, and growth of others. This mindset shift is not just beneficial for our businesses; it's a reflection of our values and character. Embracing a mindset shift, rooted in the wisdom of Philippians 2:3-4 calls us to a profound shift in perspective—one that transcends the confines of business success and reaches into the very essence of our character and values as leaders. At its core, this scripture challenges us to redefine our understanding of leadership excellence, urging us to prioritize the needs and well-being of others above our own ambitions. This then equates to service excellence as an entrepreneur. This becomes a legacy building that is sustained beyond the mundane routines of the daily self-employment grid.

To embody this ethos means leading by example and consistently demonstrating the values of humility, integrity, and compassion in our daily interactions. Each action we take, and every word we speak, reflects the depth of our character and the authenticity of our intentions. As leaders, our conduct serves as a mirror, reflecting our commitment to service excellence.

Personally, I make deliberate efforts to forge meaningful connections with my colleagues and clients, seeking to understand their challenges and extend support where needed, always with a heart devoted to service. By embracing humility and selflessness as entrepreneurs, we not only set a compelling example but also cultivate an environment where trust and loyalty flourish among employees, customers, and colleagues alike.

PRAYER FOR A SERVANT'S HEART

Gracious God,

In this moment of prayer, I humbly come before You, seeking Your divine guidance and wisdom as I navigate the journey of entrepreneurship. Grant me, O Lord, the strength and courage to lead with humility and compassion, recognizing the inherent worth and dignity of every individual I encounter along this path. Help me to embody the spirit of servant leadership, that I may serve others with grace and authenticity, reflecting Your boundless love in all my interactions.

Father, I surrender the burdens of my business into Your capable hands, trusting in Your providence and steadfast love. Grant me discernment to make decisions that honor You and benefit those around me. May Your light illuminate my path, guiding me towards opportunities for growth and prosperity, not only for myself but for all whom my business impacts.

May Your presence be my constant companion as I journey forth, filling me with courage in times of uncertainty and peace during chaos. Help me to remain steadfast in my commitment to excellence, knowing that true success lies not in worldly acclaim but in the service rendered with a sincere heart. Thank You, Lord, for the privilege of leadership. Equip me with the tools and mindset needed to excel in service, knowing that true success comes from lifting others. Make me a servant leader.

In Jesus' name, Amen.

-Dr. Angela Crutchfield,
Certified Coach and Speaker

9

SILENCE THE NOISE OF

MY CREATIVE MIND

"Be still, and know that I am God; I will be exalted among the nations, I will be exalted in the earth."
Psalm 46:10, NIV

An extrinsic concern often faced in leadership, especially as an entrepreneur, is attempting to embrace silence amidst the chaos in our often excessively busy professional and personal lives. Entrepreneurs are constantly immersed in the ever-present business demands, market dynamics, and daily pressures.

But there is an even greater intrinsic concern. Entrepreneurial leaders are not only immersed in the external demands of business but also in the ever-present whirlwind of our own creative minds. This unique aspect of entrepreneurship adds another layer to the challenge of silencing the noise to hear God's voice.

Creative minds are constantly buzzing with ideas, innovations, and possibilities. While this creativity is a valuable asset in the entrepreneurial journey, it can also become a source of distraction, overwhelm, and even behavioral health challenges. The same imaginative energy that fuels innovation can sometimes lead to a cacophony of competing thoughts and ideas, making it difficult to find stillness and clarity amid mental madness.

Amid this creative tumult, the challenge emerges—how do we quiet the internal noise to attune our spirits to God's gentle whisper? How do we sift through the multitude of ideas vying for our attention to discern the voice of divine guidance?

I've experienced firsthand the struggle of trying to silence the chatter of my own mind in order to hear God's voice clearly. In moments of inspiration and ideation, it's easy to get swept away by the excitement of new possibilities, losing sight of the quiet nudges of God's Spirit within us.

Yet, I've realized that true creativity blossoms in moments of stillness—in those sacred pauses where we allow ourselves to listen, reflect, and receive. In these moments of quiet communion with God, our creative impulses find their true direction and purpose.

As entrepreneurial leaders, we must learn to harness the power of our creative minds without allowing them to drown out the voice of God. This requires intentional practices of mindfulness, prayer, and reflection—cultivating a discipline of quieting the internal noise in order to create space for divine inspiration to flourish from deep within.

It's a journey of surrender and trust, letting go of our need for control and allowing God to guide our creative process. As we learn to quiet the busy chatter of our minds, we open ourselves up to a deeper intimacy with God and a greater clarity of vision for our entrepreneurial endeavors. In the silence, we discover a profound connection with the divine, where our hearts are attuned to the whispers of God's Spirit. As we release our firm hold on the levers of control, we find ourselves encased in a peace that surpasses understanding, guiding us with unwavering certainty along the path of divine purpose and fulfillment.

Reflecting on Psalm 46:10, we encounter the profound invitation to "Be still, and know that I am God." This verse serves as a gentle reminder that amid the constant whirlwind of our creative minds, God beckons us to pause, to quiet the incessant chatter, and to acknowledge His divine presence. When we deliberately carve out moments of silence, we create fertile ground for divine inspiration to take root and flourish.

In these sacred moments of stillness, we not only quiet the noise of our own thoughts but also open ourselves to the intrinsic voice of the Holy Spirit—a silent noise that speaks volumes in the depths of our being. As we listen to the silence, we allow this divine presence to permeate our consciousness, guiding us with wisdom and insight beyond our own understanding. It's a sacred exchange—a dance of listening and receiving, where the voice of God whispers truths and guidance into the quiet recesses of our souls.

So, let us heed the invitation of Psalm 46:10—to be still and know that He is God. Let us embrace silence as a sacred space where the noise of our own thoughts gives way to the silent whispers of the Holy Spirit. And in that sacred exchange, may we find the guidance, inspiration, and wisdom to navigate our entrepreneurial path with grace and purpose.

In our journey towards entrepreneurial success, it's paramount to prioritize the art of listening—to God's gentle whispers within that will translate to the unspoken needs of our clients. Just as we diligently seek to understand the intricate desires and challenges of our customers, we must first attune our hearts to listen deeply. By quieting the continual noise of our creative minds, we can discern the profound promptings of God's Spirit dwelling within us. This empathetic listening not only fosters innovation but also enables us to authentically connect with the genuine needs of those we serve.

PRAYER TO HEAR GOD'S VOICE

Gracious God,

Quiet my mind and tune my spirit to Your voice. On my entrepreneurial journey, I humbly come before You, recognizing the constant whirlwind of my creative mind. Lord, quiet the incessant chatter within—the myriad of ideas, doubts, and distractions that vie for attention. Still my racing thoughts and attune my spirit to the gentle whispers of Your presence. As I listen for Your guidance, may I also heed the voice deep within me, where Your Spirit resides.

Speak to the depths of my soul, O God. Let Your voice reverberate within the discord of my own ponderings. Please give me the clarity to discern Your wisdom even in the daily complexities of business and the ceaseless stream of creativity that flows within me. I am grateful for the gift of creativity, and I ask for your divine ordering of my thoughts and plans. As I seek Your guidance, may I listen intently to the silent promptings of Your Spirit dwelling within.

Grant me the grace to honor the myriad voices and perspectives that arise within my creative mind. Help me to offer clarity not only to myself but also to my clients and colleagues so that our interactions may reflect Your love and understanding.

Thank You, Lord, for entrusting me with the privilege of creativity and leadership in business. I surrender my plans and aspirations to Your perfect will. Guide me, strengthen me, and fill me with Your peace as I navigate the boundless realms of creativity each day.

In the name of Jesus,

Amen.

-Dr. Angela Crutchfield,
Certified Coach and Speaker

10

NAVIGATING THE WILDERNESS

"No Weapon formed against you shall prosper, and every tongue which rises against you in judgment You shall condemn. This is the heritage of the servants of the LORD, And their righteousness is from Me, says the LORD."
Isaiah 54:17, NKJV

As Christian entrepreneurs we want God to just make our business a success. We want to put in what we believe is hard work and expect to be blessed with success, but that is not how it works. For some of us, we must go through a process known as the wilderness season before we enter our promised land of milk of honey a.k.a. have a successful and profitable business. There are three things we should take into consideration.

First, we must ensure that our business is in line with God's purpose and will for our life.

Second, if your business is consistent with His purpose, He will prepare you to run it the way He wants it to be done. This may mean building your skill set and business knowledge over time, cleaning us up by working on your character, and ridding you of bad habits or strongholds that He knows will hinder your success.

Third, we are going to have to fight and work for it. The enemy does not want God's purpose to be fulfilled in our life. We may experience spiritual warfare. The adversary will attack you in ways you could never imagine so that you will give up, lose faith and doubt what you know God spoke over your life. He promised never to leave or forsake you and that no weapon formed against you would prosper. However, He

does not promise the weapon will not form. Therefore, we must put on our full spiritual armor and seek His protection. No matter what happens, it will always lead us back to relying on Him and not our own strength.

In this entrepreneurial journey what may hurt the most is that you will lose people that you love. God will take you through a process if you allow Him to, that will show you the true heart of those around you. You may find yourself going in circles and being delayed from walking 100% in your purpose (a successful business) until you accept this necessary purge. It will hurt, but it's all for your good. Some people cannot go with you to the next level. He heard conversations you did not hear, and He knows their hearts.

Also, God's preparation period, or the "wilderness season," will require courage, blind faith, strength, and endurance. This process is very uncomfortable. The biggest challenge will be not knowing how exactly things will unfold. Although the tasks and challenges that are a part of the preparation may appear daunting, we must remember that nothing is impossible with God and that we can do all things through Christ, who strengthens us.

PRAYER FOR YOUR WILDERNESS SEASON

Gracious God,

I pray that your will be done in my life. Please bless me with wisdom to do all that you purposed me to do when you formed me in my mother's womb. I pray for discernment to be able to distinguish between Your voice and that of the enemy. I thank you for your plans to prosper me and not to harm me, to give me hope and a future. Father, bless me so that I am surrounded by people that are in line with your purpose for my life. Remove anyone that may block me from walking fully and completely in my God Given Purpose.

Lord, bless me with the wisdom of Solomon, the courage of Esther, the faith of Abraham, the strength of Samson, and to exude the spirit of love and forgiveness as your Son, Lord Jesus, possessed when He walked the earth. If I am outside of your will, I pray that you will direct me to the right path as I know full well that Your plans are best. Lord, bless me with patience to wait on you and to not go ahead of you. I give you the authority to intercede in every aspect of my life. Guide me daily so that Your will and not my will is done in every aspect of my personal life and business. No matter what is happening in the physical world bless me to keep my eyes on you and to always possess Your peace that surpasses all understanding. In Jesus' name, amen.

-Stephanie Montgomery,
Attorney and Consultant

Surrender the Outcome

Trust God with the results, whether success or failure, knowing He is working all things together for good.

"And we know that in all things God works for the good of those who love him, who have been called according to his purpose."

– Romans 8:28

11

THE KEY TO SUCCESS IS CONSISTENCY

"We can make our own plans, but the LORD gives the right answer. ² People may be pure in their own eyes, but the LORD examines their motives. ³ Commit your actions to the LORD, and your plans will succeed."
Proverbs 16:1-3, NLT

Feeling stagnant in life can be disheartening, leading us to question our purpose and calling. We may wonder if we missed our opportunity, allowing doubt and fear to cloud our judgment. But let's remember our scripture: while we can make our own plans, God ultimately directs our steps.

Take a moment to reflect on when you first felt called by God, whether to ministry or a business venture. Are you staying true to the original call, or have you allowed distractions and doubts to alter your course? It's crucial to resist the temptation to compare ourselves to others or deviate from the path God laid out for you.

For me, my own understanding and overthinking has been a stumbling block. Case in point, I've worried about others' opinions when I've hosted events and didn't draw the expected numbers; I felt disheartened and that I have missed God. Yet, amidst the disappointment, there's a strength that keeps me persevering—it is the unwavering call from God, coupled with His grace to endure. Fulfilling God's call requires a commitment to press on despite personal feelings or perspectives. Success is found in consistent obedience. If I'm being honest, my own inconsistency has hindered my success more than anything else.

Remember, what God has assigned to you is yours alone to fulfill. Delaying obedience or attempting to replicate someone else's journey only hinders the divine purpose set before you. Whether your ministry takes place in the marketplace or within the walls of a church, it is a sacred calling, and God's guidance should be paramount in its execution. Let's commit ourselves to following God's plan faithfully, knowing His way is always best.

I know this is much easier said than done. But allow Proverbs 3:5 to be the start of all that you do. *"Lean not to your own understanding in all your ways, and let God direct your path."*

Answering the call to ministry and the marketplace often feels like a lonely journey. In those tough moments of personal struggle - trust the process. It is precisely in those hardships that our calling is refined, binding us ever closer to our purpose. It's a paradox—complex yet simple. The simplicity lies in surrendering to God's call, while the complexity lies in faithfully executing what we've heard from Him.

Isn't it incredible how God's Word supersedes our thoughts and actions? When we commit our work to the Lord, He establishes our efforts and brings our plans to fruition. Let's take a moment to praise God for His faithfulness; He alone deserves all our praise. Even when we veer off course, His divine plan still works for our ultimate good. This is the grace of God in action, turning even our wrong decisions into right outcomes.

If you feel like you've missed your opportunity, let me encourage you: You're on God's timetable. His plans are designed to prosper you and lead you to guaranteed success—no ifs, ands, or buts. The key is to fully surrender to His call.

Now, you might be wondering, "How do I surrender completely and swiftly?" The answer lies in obeying the promptings of your heart.

Move quickly, and you'll witness God's hand at work in your life. Every step you take will be marked by His favor, but remember: *the favor comes after action.* Trust me; as you step out in faith, you'll receive the help you need to fulfill God's call on your life. So, take heart, be encouraged, and move swiftly in obedience to what God has said. Let us pray.

PRAYER FOR SUCCESS

Gracious God,

Thank You for entrusting me with another chance to serve You. I humbly ask for Your forgiveness for doubting Your plan for my life. Today, I recommit my plans into Your hands, surrendering to Your divine guidance. Please grant me the grace to navigate through challenges with unwavering passion, always keeping my eyes fixed on You as the ultimate author and finisher of my fate. I trust Your plans wholeheartedly, knowing that You alone know what's best for me.

Lead me, Lord, to divine partnerships, and guide me away from any connections that may hinder Your purpose for my life. Keep my heart soft and open to Your leading. May my YES to the call be blessed with continual growth and prosperity, all as a result of my obedience to You.

In Jesus' name, I pray. Amen.

-Dr. Patrice May, *Author,*
TV Host and Speaker

12

UNLEASH YOUR INNER POWER

"And we know that God causes all things to work together for good to those who love God, to those who are called according to His purpose."
Romans 8:28 NASB

In the depths of my entrepreneurial journey, I faced a relentless onslaught of challenges that threatened to consume me. Marketing woes weighed heavily on my shoulders, and the struggle to attract consistent clients felt like an uphill battle. Each day seemed to blur into the next as I navigated the labyrinth of entrepreneurship with a heavy heart and weary spirit.

When it comes to marketing, the struggle is real. Do you market on Facebook, Instagram, or other social media platforms? Should you hire a marketing company, even if it means spending money you haven't earned yet? And if you decide to do the marketing yourself, do you have the structure, time, and dedication to make it work? Let's keep it real - what are you marketing, and who can you trust for the right advice? It feels like everyone out there has a scheme, and you've tried programs and investing money without getting the results you expected. Marketing isn't just about which social media platforms to use or how much money to spend. It's about defining your company's vision and understanding your niche market. Have you considered if this aligns with your values and what you believe God wants for you? The Bible advises against boasting and encourages us to be wise with our resources. Are you investing your money in a way that pleases God? It's important to consider if your marketing efforts are in line with your values and if you're being wise with your resources. Additionally, it's crucial to establish a marketing schedule to keep things on track.

Let me be real with you: the other parts are the clients. You get a client and feel excited, but then you realize you need to find more clients and are unsure how to do it. It's a lot to navigate. I've learned that instead of worrying about how to market, I need to understand what God wants from me and what will work best. Understanding my finances and my past has helped me find clarity. When I embraced what I needed to do, I started seeking the right resources to achieve my goals. I was looking in the wrong places and trusting the wrong sources. If your business is based on faith, then turn to God for guidance. I started asking God to connect me with the right business coach, resources, and courses, and that's exactly what happened.

The greatest breakthroughs often stem from the greatest struggles.

Let's be honest—when it comes to marketing, I initially approached my projects with a belief that success would come naturally. I thought having a great idea that solves a problem would be enough, and people would just flock to it. But that mindset was a misconception. One of the biggest challenges in entrepreneurship is the notion that success comes without proper planning or research.

In my journey, I've learned the hard way that you must plan your work and work your plan. Marketing is a crucial aspect of any business; neglecting it can be detrimental. Let's start with some practical advice: don't embark on a creative venture without thorough research and a well-thought-out budget. I've found that 50% of my budget often goes into advertising—whether it's consulting with a website expert or investing in social media ads.

Now, let's bring this into a Christian perspective. God has gifted you with your idea and your assignment. As it says in Romans 8:28, *"And we know that in all things God works for the good of those who love him, who have been called according to his purpose."* The resources and knowledge you need will come if you seek the right sources and start with a strong foundation in God.

Here's how I turned my marketing challenges around:

1. **Start with Yourself**: Ensure your relationship with God is strong. I focused on transforming my mind and ensuring intimacy with God was a priority over financial gain.

2. **Seek Wisdom**: Pray for wisdom in your business endeavors, just as Solomon did. Ask God to show you how to run your business with wisdom and to direct you to the right resources and people.

3. **Consult Experts**: God has gifted others with expertise that can help you. I partnered with a publisher and a business coach who guided me through understanding my identity, niche, and marketing strategies.

4. **Leverage Social Media**: Experiment with social media, follow trends, and stay true to your assignment. I didn't just buy Facebook ads; I focused on posting meaningful content that aligned with my mission.

5. **Embrace Collaboration**: When God brings the right people into your life, they will complement your strengths and fill in your gaps. Together, you will create something beautiful that glorifies God and fulfills your purpose.

Practical Steps for You:

1. **Pause and Reflect**: Take 24-48 hours or even a week to deepen your relationship with God. Study scripture, pray, and journal your thoughts and frustrations.

2. **Seek Clarity**: Write out your problems and ask God-specific questions. You have not because you ask not.

3. **Ensure Your Heart is Right**: Understand your purpose and who your clients are. Ensure your motives are aligned with God's calling, not just financial gain.

4. **Submit to God's Will**: Trust that if you put God first, everything you need will follow. You must do the work, but God will guide you to the right people and opportunities.

Remember, everything works together for good when you are focused on God's plan for you. You'll recognize the right people by their alignment with God's principles and their honest truth.

In conclusion, my journey from marketing woes to success was built on a foundation of faith, wisdom, and collaboration. As I prepare for my fourth book, I see God's hand in every connection and every decision. Trust Him, do the work, and you will see His promises fulfilled in your business.

PRAYER FOR INNER POWER

Gracious God, in the depths of my soul, I cry out to You, seeking solace and divine intervention in my entrepreneurial journey. As I navigate the tumultuous seas of business, I am confronted with challenges that threaten to overwhelm me. Yet, I cling to the promise of your Word, knowing that you are the ultimate architect of my destiny.

Father, cleanse my heart of doubt and fear and renew my spirit with unwavering faith. Grant me the fortitude to press on when the path seems obscured and the courage to persevere when the storms rage fiercely. May Your presence be my guiding light, illuminating the darkest corners of uncertainty and leading me to the shores of victory.

Lord, I surrender my business into your hands, trusting in your divine plan and timing. May every endeavor I undertake be infused with your wisdom and grace, bearing fruit that glorifies your holy name. In Jesus' mighty name, I pray. Amen.

-Natasha Richards,
Author, Pastor, and Coach

Pray for Integrity and Ethical Practices

Ask for the strength to operate your business with honesty and fairness, even when it's challenging.

"And what does the Lord require of you? To act justly and to love mercy and to walk humbly with your God."

– Micah 6:8

13

MANAGE PEOPLE WITH PURPOSE

"Come, follow me," Jesus said, "and I will send you out to fish for people." Immediately, they left their nets and followed him."
Mark 1:17-18, NKJV

In the world of business, it is essential to discern the differences between the qualities of an exceptional leader and those of an exceptional manager. Leadership can be defined as the art of guiding a group of individuals or an entire organization, while management involves overseeing and coordinating resources, tasks, and people. The challenge lies in knowing when to assume each role and, at times, when it is necessary to fulfill both roles concurrently. This section of the book will briefly focus on the principles of management. In the scripture text above, Jesus, as the Supreme Leader, imparts three principles of great management as He begins to assemble His management team (a.k.a. His disciples).

The first factor is "Call," which can also be seen as the "Who and/ or How." As a manager, it's crucial to make the best decision on who or what you will use to help you achieve your goals. Knowing your goals is essential in determining the best people and resources to help you reach them. This applies to every aspect of a manager's recruitment, hiring, and termination process. When Jesus invited them to come, there was no mistaking whom He was talking to; He was clear and direct.

Colossians 3:23 (NLT) "Work willingly at whatever you do, as though you were working for the Lord rather than for people."

The next crucial step in becoming an effective manager is consistently demonstrating your character and values. It is essential to build trust in relationships and handle resources with integrity. Doing so will make it easier for people to have confidence in you and support your plans. Similar to the disciples that Jesus called, who were able to trust and follow Him because of His character, it is important to be recognized as someone who is reliable and trustworthy.

1 Corinthians 4:2 (NLT), A good manager must be faithful and reliable.

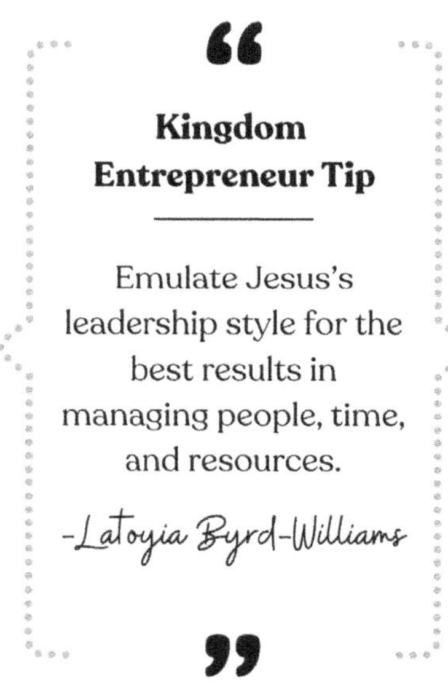

Last but not least, it's important to have clarity about the "When," which means knowing when things need to be done. Are the expectations clearly defined in terms of what needs to be accomplished and when? In the context of our main scripture text, Jesus had a clear understanding of the assignment, which was "to fish for people." It's crucial to ensure that when you're seeking to accomplish a task, you communicate the end goal clearly to all involved parties in order to equip the team for success. Remember Brene Brown's quote from "Dare to Lead," "Clear is kind. Unclear is unkind."

As these three principles were present in the life of Jesus, it resulted in an immediate response to the call. It's important for you as a manager to consider the following principles as you refine, test, and adjust your management tools. First, consider the question, *"Whom do people say that you are?"* This question serves as a simple exercise for you to assess how you are perceived by both your superiors and your subordinates. Understanding others' perceptions of you can potentially make the management process smoother. Have you ever found yourself struggling to complete a task without a clear understanding of what you're supposed to do and why it's important? How did this lack of clarity make you feel? It's crucial to ensure that your objectives are well-defined and meet the criteria of being specific, measurable, achievable, relevant, and time-bound—commonly known as SMART goals.

PRAYER FOR MANAGING PEOPLE

God, I thank You for the opportunity to manage Your people whether in the workplace, in my business, at home, or in ministry. May You guide me so I can guide others according to Your Word and Your Way! As I manage Your people, allow me to see it as ministry so that it isn't a burden, and I can be a witness and a blessing. Allow me to do it with gratitude and understanding, being a peacemaker rather than a peace lover, making Your Name great among men. I want to be a manager that others want to follow with immediacy and hunger to accomplish Your purpose and Your plan. In Jesus Name, Amen!

- Latoyia Byrd-Williams,
Author, Book Editor and Consultant

Intercede for Employees and Clients

Pray for the well-being, growth, and success of your team, clients, and anyone impacted by your business.

"Carry each other's burdens, and in this way, you will fulfill the law of Christ."

– Galatians 6:2

14

DIVINE COLLABORATIONS

"Trust in the Lord with all your heart and lean not on your own understanding; in all your ways submit to Him, and He will make your paths straight." Proverbs 3:5-6

In the world of entrepreneurship, few decisions hold as much weight as choosing the right business partner. A partnership can either amplify your success or lead to unforeseen challenges, making it essential to approach this decision with both wisdom and discernment. Just as God calls us to be intentional with every aspect of our lives, He also expects us to be intentional about who we join forces within business.

Discernment in Business Partnerships

The Bible teaches us to seek discernment in all things, and this is especially true when it comes to choosing business partners. Proverbs 3:5-6 says, *"Trust in the Lord with all your heart and lean not on your own understanding; in all your ways submit to Him, and He will make your paths straight."* This passage reminds us that our judgment alone is insufficient. We must seek God's wisdom and guidance in our decisions, particularly in something as significant as a partnership.

Business partners do more than share in financial responsibilities; they share your vision. The vision God has given you is sacred. It is not merely a business strategy but a divine purpose that He has entrusted to you. When you consider partnering with someone, you invite them into this space, asking them to contribute to fulfilling that God-given purpose. This is why discernment is essential.

The Role of Prayer

Prayer must be at the center of every partnership decision. Before you enter any agreement or align yourself with another person's skills, talents, or financial backing, you must first align your heart with God's will. Philippians 4:6 says, *"Do not be anxious about anything, but in every situation, by prayer and petition, with thanksgiving, present your requests to God."*

Pray for guidance, clarity, and peace about the individuals you are considering working with. Ask God to reveal any red flags, show you their true character, and confirm whether this person is meant to walk alongside you in the journey of entrepreneurship. Trust that He will guide you through the Holy Spirit, who gives wisdom to those who seek it earnestly.

Shared Values and Vision

It is important to partner with someone whose values and integrity align with yours. Amos 3:3 asks, *"Can two walk together, except they be agreed?"* A successful business partnership is built on shared beliefs and a common vision. You and your partner must have a mutual understanding of the mission God has placed on your hearts and agree on the principles that will guide the business.

In the same way that light cannot mix with darkness, you cannot partner with someone who lacks integrity, transparency, or a strong moral compass. If there are misalignments in core values, it will inevitably lead to conflict and potential harm to your business. Before moving forward, seek to understand whether your partner shares your commitment to honesty, fairness, and ethical business practices.

Knowing When to Say No

There may be times when the temptation to partner with someone is strong. Perhaps they have the financial backing, industry connections, or experience you lack. But if God has not given you peace about this partnership, it is important to walk away. Saying "no" to the wrong partnership can save you from countless headaches, legal battles, and heartache in the future.

Remember, it's not about how skilled or experienced a potential partner may be. It's about whether they align with God's will for your business. When you rely on prayer and discernment, you may find that God leads you to partners who not only help your business grow but also encourage and strengthen your faith along the way.

The Importance of Accountability

Finally, business partnerships thrive when there is a sense of accountability. You should trust your partner to uphold their responsibilities and hold each other accountable to the vision God has given you. This requires open communication, humility, and a willingness to correct each other in love when needed.

Godly business partners pray together, seek God's wisdom together, and remain open to His correction. They understand that they are stewards of something much bigger than themselves. A successful business is not just measured by profit but by how well it aligns with God's will and purposes.

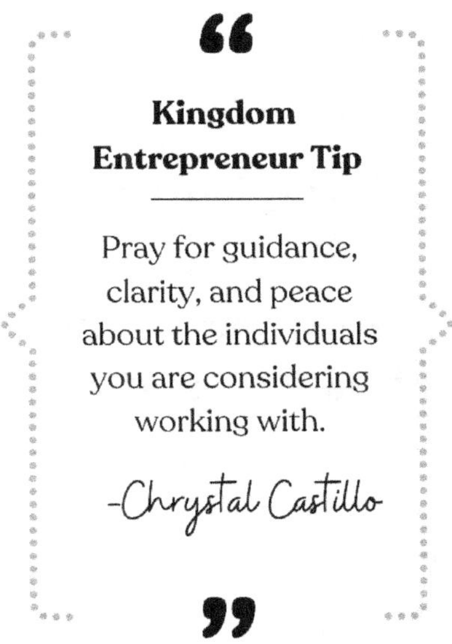

Conclusion

Choosing a business partner is a significant step in entrepreneurship, and it should never be taken lightly. By seeking God's guidance in prayer, exercising discernment, and ensuring that your partner shares your vision and values, you can form a partnership that honors God and furthers His purpose for your business.

As you navigate the path of entrepreneurship, trust that God will provide the right people at the right time. Seek His wisdom above all else, and remember that your business is ultimately His.

PRAYER PRINCIPLE

Ask for Protection and Provision

Pray for God's protection over your business, finances, and reputation, and trust Him to provide what you need.

"And my God will meet all your needs according to the riches of his glory in Christ Jesus."

– Philippians 4:19

PRAYER FOR DISCERNMENT IN BUSINESS PARTNERSHIPS

Heavenly Father,

I come before You today with a heart seeking wisdom and clarity in my business partnerships. Lord, You are the Author of all things, the source of divine insight and understanding. I ask that You guide me in every decision I make, especially in the connections I form with others in business.

Lord, as I seek to build and collaborate, may I be discerning and recognize the partnerships that align with Your will. Let my decisions be rooted in righteousness, integrity, and mutual respect. Help me to see beyond the surface, discerning the intentions and values of those I am considering working with.

Grant me the patience to listen for Your voice and the courage to step away from any partnership that does not honor You or lead to a greater purpose. Bless those I collaborate with, that together we may create, innovate, and serve for the greater good.

Help me to trust in Your divine timing, knowing that You will bring the right people into my life at the right moment. May our collaborations reflect Your love, bring glory to Your name, and bear fruit that is abundant and lasting.

In all that I do, may I remain humble and open to Your leading, recognizing that true success comes from aligning my will with Yours.

In Jesus' name, I pray, Amen.

-**Chrystal Castillo**, *Author,*
Literary Engineer and Grant Writer

Pray for Creativity and Innovation

Seek God's inspiration for fresh ideas, solutions, and strategies that set your business apart.

"For we are God's handiwork, created in Christ Jesus to do good works, which God prepared in advance for us to do."

– Ephesians 2:10

15

TRUSTING GOD

"A father to the fatherless, a defender of widows,
is God in His holy dwelling."
Psalm 68:5, NIV

As a single parent, I used to wonder how I could manage all this in a 24-hour day: make sure my children's needs were met, balance a job, and start the business I have been thinking about for quite some time now. Can I share with you a part of my life story and how I made it through?

The journey was not easy to say the least. Having my first child at eighteen and then two more after that, I had my hands full. After a failed marriage, I found myself trying to take care of three children on my own, so what was I to do? And what was God's role in that?

Psalm 68:5a (NIV) says that He is a father to the fatherless. Although you may feel like you are alone, know that God is your Father as well as your children's father. His word says, *"I will never leave you nor forsake you."* Hebrews 13:5b (KJV), and so I had to lean on the guidance of the Holy Spirit in raising my three children.

I learned to lean on the Lord with all my heart and mind, trusting and having confidence in Him. I acknowledge Him in everything concerning me, trusting Him to guide my paths so that I would not stumble along the way, Proverbs 3:5, 6 (paraphrased).

I started trusting in God even though sometimes it was hard, especially when we did not have enough food. One time, things were so bad; in order for us to make it, I decided to go on a fast and give the food to my children. God was so good that He provided me with food the next

day. We had enough to last until our food stamps arrived. I was on welfare, and in those days, we did not have food stamp cards; we used the paper booklets-you know, the ones that had singles, fives, and tens that looked like monopoly money. Here I was, trying to take care of three children, depending on God as my source.

You can make It!

Psalm 34:4 (ESV) says, I sought the Lord, and He answered me; He delivered me from all my fears. Today, I am an established Author of four books, *Say It Til You See It, Jealous Sisters, He's A Father To The Fatherless, and His Dark Side*, songwriter and business owner of Agape Catering and Cake service, and I contribute it all to the Almighty God.

Regardless of your beginnings, don't let what you are going through stop you from pursuing your desires, passion, and dreams for your future. God is no respecter of persons. Romans 2:11 reminds us that what He has done for me, He will do for you as well.

PRAYER FOR TRUSTING GOD

Gracious God, my Lord and Savior, you have been a stronghold to me when I was in trouble. I thank you for your guidance, for being that strong tower that I could run to and hide myself until I regained my strength. You said in your Word that if I acknowledged you in all my ways, you would make my path clear, and so I submit everything to you: my businesses, my ministry, my family, and even my health. Bless them all and enlarge my territory.

Thank you for being right here with me, even in the midst of those storms that tried to pull me under. You gave me an anchor that kept me from going under and led me to a place of peace. Your rod and staff have comforted me, and I have rested beside a quiet stream. You taught me strategies and gave me insight on how to gain wealth, and my vision is clear.

Thank you to the destiny helpers you brought into my life to help me in areas where I needed help. You knew who I needed in my life for such a time as this, and your eyes are ever on me to keep me going in the right direction. Surely, your goodness and mercy shall follow me all the days of my life, and I will forever dwell in your house and continue to give you praise, in Jesus' name.

- Brenda Burton,
Author, Songwriter and
Entrepreneur

Stay Grateful and Humble

Thank God for the opportunities, resources, and lessons your business journey provides.

"Give thanks in all circumstances; for this is God's will for you in Christ Jesus."

– 1 Thessalonians 5:18

16

STEP OUT OF THE BOAT

"For we live by faith, not by sight."
2 Corinthians 5:7, NIV

In 2018, I spent almost 17 years with one corporate team in the world of financial services. I worked with one of the largest teams in the country in terms of both assets under management and revenue. We were consistently ranked as a top team in the country by respected publications. After all that time with one team, I did not know what the outside world looked like. I only knew how one team had functioned in wealth management. I knew the ins and outs. Add to the fact that in 2018, I hit a peak income year.

Then, in late 2018, the Lord clearly told me a change was coming. I thought it meant going to work for another large team, and I was both excited and nervous at the thought. But I was ready for a change and had been asking God for years to open a new door. What I did not realize was that the direction was one that I least expected: the road to entrepreneurship and building a financial services firm from scratch. That was not a part of my plan. It was not even a thought if I were being honest. And yet, my directions were clear in the only door that was opened.

Being an entrepreneur as a financial advisor did not quite make sense for the period of life I was in. This is one of the hardest businesses to build, and most people who do it either do not have a family to support yet, or they had a spouse who would be able to cover the bills while the business got off the ground, which often took years to do so.

I was a divorced, single mom with a mortgage. As a Black Woman CFP(r) and CPA, I also represented less than 1% of the whole financial service profession. There was nothing usual about my path.

As the Lord started drawing me closer to Him, or in reality, I started wanting to hear more of what God had to say, I stumbled upon Dr. Charles Stanley and his simple way of sharing the message in a powerful way. One of the things he shared often was "obey God and leave the consequences to Him". As I grew more in following Jesus, my instructions never entirely made sense to me. I would be asked to do things that were always out of my league and things I would never tell myself to do. I was asked to write publicly. I started journaling some of my frustrations, and God told me I should write for an audience. "Hmmm. No, thank you." Of course, my decline did not change my instruction.

In late summer 2018, I published my first devotional, *"Walking By Faith, and Not By Sight: Learning to Be Still in the Midst of Life's Chaos."* I had been walking by faith and not by sight, and God was ready for me to take the next steps. It's almost as if He was ready to confirm whether I would use what I had been learning. He put me to the test, and by Fall 2018, He told me it was time to leave. By this time, I had been developing a track record with Him. He had taken a non-writer and turned me into a published author, and the way He had done it was nothing short of a miracle. So, when I was told it was time to leave, I knew I had to do like Abraham and start walking. Honestly, I had no idea what my life would look like. There were very few examples of people that I knew who were doing this crazy faith thing that God was asking me to do. And yet, I knew my job was to "walk by faith, and not by sight" and to "obey God and leave all the consequences to Him."

I was once asked what my backup plan was, and my response was "there is no backup plan." It hadn't even occurred to me that I should have had a backup plan, not because I was being irresponsible but because I believed with my whole heart that God had called me to this space, and He would make the way, even when there seemed to be no way.

As of the writing of this, I have celebrated five years as an independent financial advisor. I can now see that the first call was just a stepping stone to the next call, which was to open my own financial services firm. God, in His infinite wisdom, knew that I would not have been able to leave straight from corporate to opening my own firm, so He allowed me to take an intermediary step. I thought it was a permanent place, but after only two years, God said that it was just a stop.

One of the most amazing things is that He allowed my obedience in 2018 and doing all the things to create a company to become the stepping stone to launching my financial services firm, Kaysi Gordon Financial Planning, in 2022. One piece of the puzzle was necessary to get to the next, and it was accomplished by obedience.

Friends, when God tells you to get out of the boat, get out of the boat in faith and obedience.

PRAYER FOR FAITH

Gracious God,

I am so grateful that you saw fit to call me to this space in this time period. Thank you for allowing me to do the things that you have. Father, I admit that it has not been easy, but I can see that you have been with me every step of the way. You have filled me with encouragement and hope. You have provided for all my needs, according to your riches in glory. Father, as others may be struggling with whether you have called them to entrepreneurship, I ask that you give them clarity. Allow them to step out in faith so that they too can experience your blessings. In Jesus' name. Amen

-Kaysian C. Gordon,
Author, Financial Advisor,
Speaker and Bible Teacher

17

GODLY STRATEGIC DECISIONS

"The LORD Himself goes before you and will be with you; He will never leave you nor forsake you. Do not be afraid; do not be discouraged."
Deuteronomy 31:8, NIV

There will come a time in every entrepreneur's life when one of two things will happen in their business. The first thing is they will peak in their business. This occurs when one has a unique niche (product or service) that answers a problem. The issue becomes, what happens when you peak and plateau? Meaning, that it looks like you've exhausted your niche and solved the problem, and now you've run out of clients to sell to or serve.

The other thing that happens to entrepreneurs is they will fall flat in their business. This means they may have a great concept or idea, but the execution to bring that concept or idea to life doesn't gain traction, resulting in a lack of clients or sales. When an entrepreneur hits this "wall," sometimes we become discouraged, especially when we see other entrepreneurs flourishing in the same industry.

I started my brand in 2011 with a unique story. My brand was created to provide natural skincare and hair care and create an atmosphere that fosters self-care and an environment of wellness. This is my niche and helps to solve a problem. I was in business for 9 years before I saw some traction in sales. During the pandemic in 2020, I experienced my best year; this was mainly because I was predominantly e-commerce, and with the world being shut down, I was able to fill a need many had, which was to stock up on personal items, while creating a spa-like atmosphere in their homes (especially with the stress we were experiencing due to Covid-19). As the pandemic ended and the world returned to a sense of normalcy, I celebrated ten years in business in 2011 with a pop-up store in a brick-and-mortar. My business softened in the e-commerce space and soared to its peak in-store due to in-person sales. At the height of my business, I was called to return to the office at my 9-5 corporate job.

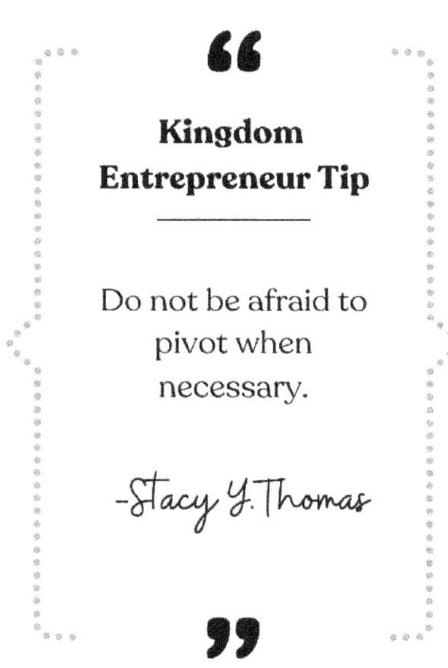

Unfortunately, this change affected my relationship with the business I was partnering with, and I eventually exited that retail space.

Instead of being upset about the changes, I had to realize that seasons change in business, whether it be the business itself, the timing and climate of the world, or the partnerships you enter. I took my experiences in that retail space and learned from the lessons, but I had to PIVOT in my business model. I lost a lot of money because of the change, so I needed guidance on how to get my business back to the revenue I was accruing in 2020 and 2021. The first thing I did was ask God for clarity about the past season in my business. Secondly, I prayed for direction. I asked God to literally go before me, clear the path, and *lead me* in getting my business back on track. I doubled down and started to increase my engagement online and marketing emails. I also stepped out on faith and participated in vendor events in areas I was not familiar with. I eventually increased my e-commerce engagement, which increased sales, and created a broader customer base by expanding my network and reach in different markets.

The entrepreneur's life has its ups and downs, ebbs and flows. If you're going to be in it for the long haul, you have to be able to adapt to change. You cannot be scared of it. Change provides the opportunity to pivot. Pivoting offers the opportunity to create freshness in your business, possibly an untapped niche and/or another income stream. Change does not equal failure. I found that the best way to avoid the trick of feeling defeated when you need to pivot is to stay connected to the Holy Spirit. Be attentive and discerning when you see the signs of impending change, and don't ignore the nudging of the Holy Spirit. God will go before you in your business, will be with you on your entrepreneurial journey, and He will not leave you, especially during challenging times. When those difficult times come, do not be afraid or discouraged! Pray, listen for an answer, strategize, execute, and watch God work!

PRAYER FOR PIVOTS

Gracious God,

I thank you for the gifts and talents you've blessed me with. Thank you for allowing me to turn those gifts and talents into a viable business. Father, sometimes I don't feel I am doing enough business. I feel like I should and could be doing better and greater, but I don't know where to start. I don't know how to shift when my sales and revenue fall flat. When I experience mental roadblocks, I don't know how to get out of the rut of feeling unaccomplished. When I am not motivated, I fight to get motivated again.

Regardless of how I feel, I know Your Word says that You will never leave me nor forsake me. Even when I don't understand what is happening in my business, I know You're right there with me. So, God, I ask that when changes need to be made in my business, You open my eyes to see where I need to pivot. When I am feeling unaccomplished or hit a proverbial brick wall, encourage my heart, reminding me that You created me for my business and placed everything in me to succeed. When my heart is overwhelmed, may I always consult with You for divine direction. Fear and discouragement have no place in my business. I will pivot when necessary, with confidence and boldness, because You have already gone before me to clear the path and provide provision... and for that, I THANK YOU.

In Jesus' name, amen.

-Stacy Y. Thomas,
Author of Single-ish and Where Do I Go From Here?, Beauty Entrepreneur and Speaker

ENTREPRENEURS BLUEPRINT

FOR SUCCESS

"I can do all things through Christ who strengthens me."
Ephesians 4:13

As an entrepreneur, the path to success is often fraught with challenges that test your resolve, faith, and perseverance. Among these obstacles, five critical barriers—doubt, discouragement, diversion, defeat, and delay—can significantly impede your progress and diminish your spirit. Recognizing and addressing these "Five D's" is essential for maintaining your focus and achieving your entrepreneurial dreams. This chapter offers practical advice rooted in biblical wisdom to help you overcome these common pitfalls. By embracing these strategies, you can strengthen your faith, enhance your resilience, and navigate the entrepreneurial journey with confidence and purpose.

THE FIVE D'S FOR ENTREPRENEURS

1. Doubt: The Silent Saboteur

Doubt makes you question God's Word and His goodness. As an entrepreneur, doubt is not an option. When it arises, surround yourself with the Word of God and His promises. Remember, there's no person, thing, or circumstance that should ever make you question God's provision, love, forgiveness, grace, and mercy.

"But when you ask, you must believe and not doubt, because the one who doubts is like a wave of the sea, blown and tossed by the wind." - James 1:6

Practical Application:

Create a daily affirmation routine. Start each day by reading and meditating on Bible verses that affirm God's promises and your purpose. Keep a journal to record instances where you've seen God's hand in your business to remind yourself of His faithfulness during moments of doubt.

2. Discouragement: The Perspective Shifter

Discouragement makes you focus on your problems rather than on God. You can't look up while looking down. Keep your eyes on God's hand in your storms, not on the size of your problems. Understand that it's not about how big your problems are, but about recognizing how big God is.

"Have I not commanded you? Be strong and courageous. Do not be afraid; do not be discouraged, for the Lord your God will be with you wherever you go." - Joshua 1:9

Practical Application:

Set up regular "gratitude breaks" throughout your day. Take a few moments to thank God for His blessings and to reflect on how He has helped you overcome previous challenges. Keeping a gratitude journal can also help maintain a positive outlook and keep discouragement at bay.

3. Diversion: The False Attraction

Diversion makes the wrong things seem attractive, tempting you to desire them more than the right things. In sports and the military, diversion tactics are common. As an entrepreneur, ensure your mind, heart, and soul are armed with the Word of God and His love, avoiding wrong environments, dramas, or problems.

"Do not love the world or anything in the world. If anyone loves the world, love for the Father is not in them." - 1 John 2:15

Practical Application:

Identify and avoid your major distractions. Make a list of activities or environments that divert your attention from your business goals. Create a disciplined schedule that prioritizes your main tasks and includes regular spiritual practices to keep you focused on God's will for your business.

4. Defeat: The Paralyzing Feeling

Defeat makes you feel like a failure, discouraging you from trying. Build a foundation that prevents you from feeling defeated. Every detail matters, from your environment to your inner circle. When you feel defeated, ask yourself: Why do you feel this way? Who says you are defeated? What lesson can you learn in this valley? What does the Bible say about defeat?

"For though the righteous fall seven times, they rise again, but the wicked stumble when calamity strikes." - Proverbs 24:16

Kingdom Entrepreneur Tip

Stay laser-focused on your purpose.

-Natasha Richards

Practical Application:

Develop a support network. Surround yourself with mentors, peers, and friends who encourage you and hold you accountable. When feeling defeated, seek their counsel and prayer. Reflect on past successes and lessons learned from failures to reinforce your resilience.

5. Delay: The Productivity Killer

Delay, often seen as procrastination, makes you put off tasks so that they never get done. When you delay, have a plan to return to and focus on the task. It's more important to do one thing well than to attempt 25 different things at once. Master one thing, letting your clients know you're the best at it, and then expand.

"The plans of the diligent lead to profit as surely as haste leads to poverty."
- Proverbs 21:5

Practical Application:

Implement the "One Task" rule. Each day, identify the single most important task that will move your business forward and commit to completing it before focusing on anything else. Use tools like time-blocking and project management software to keep track of your tasks and deadlines, ensuring steady progress.

PRAYER FOR SUCCESS

Dear Heavenly Father,

As I reflect on my journey as an entrepreneur, I am aware of the numerous challenges and obstacles that may hinder my success. I come to you seeking your guidance and the strength to remain focused. I ask for courage and persistence as I navigate through the uncertainties and potential pitfalls. Please help me to align my thoughts and actions with your will.

I pray for your protection over my mind and thoughts, so that I may make decisions that are reflective of your divine presence within me. Grant me the wisdom to build a character that mirrors your grace and love. Help me to remain steadfast in my faith, even in the face of distractions and challenges. May your guidance be a constant reminder of your presence in my endeavors.

I ask for your blessing and protection over my business and over my life. In Jesus' name, I pray. Amen.

-Natasha Richards,
Author of For the Levites and Mindset Reset,
Coach and Pastor

Be Bold in Faith

Pray boldly for growth, favor, and impact, knowing God is able to do exceedingly abundantly above all you can ask or imagine.

"Now to him who is able to do immeasurably more than all we ask or imagine, according to his power that is at work within us."

– Ephesians 3:20

19

RESTING IN BUSINESS

"There is a time for everything, and a season for every activity under the heavens."
Ecclesiastes 3:1

One of the most challenging cycles I had to break in my business was the belief that I needed to work 8 hours a day, 5 days a week. I started in corporate America at 17, and this mindset was all I knew. But in reality, forcing myself into an 8-hour workday stifled my creativity and ingenuity while significantly increasing my stress levels. This approach also contributed to weight gain from sitting for prolonged periods. It wasn't that I couldn't exercise—I felt guilty taking time away from work to do it.

I even stopped attending my favorite workout studio because I calculated that the travel and exercise time carved too much out of my workday. Instead of focusing on what I was gaining from working out, I fixated on what I was giving up. This thought process prioritized work over my health. As a full-time entrepreneur, it's admittedly hard to achieve balance. If you don't work, you don't eat. The stakes are even higher when you have a family, mortgage, and other financial responsibilities. We often believe that the harder we work, the more valuable we are to our business and family.

However, I've learned that neglecting our well-being makes us less valuable to everyone around us. One of the greatest lessons I've embraced is that balance is impossible without boundaries. For me, this meant

setting clear boundaries with clients. I established specific work hours and made it a rule not to respond to emails, calls, or texts outside those hours. I used to get calls at 10 p.m., like a doctor on call! Surprisingly, enforcing boundaries with clients was easier than setting boundaries for my self-care and well-being.

To combat this, I designated Fridays as my self-care day. I use it for things like hair and nail appointments, breakfast with friends, or even just lounging on the couch without my phone, catching up on my favorite shows. Sometimes, I don't do anything until the kids get home from school, and then I transform into a pumpkin or what I call "Mom mode."

REST IS BIBLICAL

Rest is biblical, and it must be part of your business plan. In Genesis, God Himself rested on the seventh day, setting an example for us to follow (*Genesis 2:2-3*). The command to observe the Sabbath in *Exodus 20:8-10* underscores the importance of rest, not just for physical rejuvenation but as an act of trust in God. When we rest, we acknowledge that God is the ultimate provider and sustainer of all our efforts.

Jesus also emphasized the need for rest, demonstrating it in His own life. In *Mark 6:31*, He encouraged His disciples to "come away by yourselves to a secluded place and rest a while." Rest allows us to realign our priorities, refresh our minds, and refocus on God's purposes. By incorporating rest into your business and life, you honor God's design and create space for Him to work in and through you.

Failing to rest often leads to burnout, frustration, and ineffectiveness. Without intentional moments of rest, you are sabotaging your business, family, and ministry life. Rest isn't optional; it's essential for sustaining the roles God has called you to fulfill. By including rest in your business plan, you're not only preserving your health and well-being but also demonstrating faith in God's ability to provide even when you pause your labor.

INCORPORATING REST

Create a self-care day and commit to protecting it as a non-negotiable boundary in your life. Start by identifying a day or specific time in your week that you can dedicate solely to self-care or rest. This doesn't have to look the same for everyone—it should reflect what restores and energizes you. It could be:

- Spending time in prayer, worship, or journaling to connect with God.

- Going for a walk, exercising, or taking a class to nourish your body.

- Enjoying quiet moments with a good book, catching up on your favorite shows, or simply doing nothing.

- Scheduling appointments for things like hair, nails, or a massage to refresh yourself physically.

- Having quality time with family or close friends without interruptions from work.

Guard this time fiercely. Treat it as a sacred appointment you wouldn't dream of canceling. Let clients, colleagues, and family members know that this time is set aside and non-negotiable. Consider adding it to your calendar or daily planner as a recurring event to remind yourself of its importance.

Remember, rest and self-care aren't selfish—they're necessary. Investing in your well-being makes you better equipped to serve your business, family, and ministry.

PRAYER FOR REST

Heavenly Father,

Thank You for the precious gift of rest, a reminder of Your care and provision for me. You have shown through Your Word and example that rest is not a weakness but a blessing—a time to refresh, realign, and restore. Help me to see rest not as something I must earn but as a sacred rhythm You've designed for my life.

Lord, I ask for Your wisdom as I navigate the responsibilities of my family, business, and ministry. Teach me to embrace balance, knowing that my time and capacity are ultimately gifts from You. Help me to set healthy boundaries that protect the space I need for rest and renewal so I can reflect Your peace and joy in all that I do.

Father, remind me daily that my worth is not tied to my productivity or achievements but solely to Your love for me. Help me to release the pressure to prove myself and instead lean into the truth that I am already enough in Christ.

Grant me the discipline and courage to prioritize self-care, not out of selfishness, but as an act of stewardship over the body, mind, and spirit You've entrusted to me. Show me how to use my moments of rest to draw closer to You, to deepen my relationships with my loved ones, and to regain the strength I need to serve others with excellence.

In Jesus' name, I pray, Amen.

-Athena C. Shack, *Author of Grace for the Journey, Becoming God's Dwelling Place, CEO of Watersprings Publishing, and Speaker*

ABOUT THE AUTHORS

TASHA BARON SMITH, a dedicated Navy spouse and mother of four, holds a Bachelor of Science in Business Administration with a concentration in Accounting and Strategic Management. Her ambitious and solution-driven mindset has not only brought success to her own endeavors but also to her family and every client she partners with. She is passionate about  helping others realize their personal power and identity. As a Mentor and Life-Strategist, she provides strategic planning and support, guiding individuals to uncover their true potential and ignite the passion within them to move forward. Her personal mission is to help others discover who they truly are and inspire them to break free from stagnation.

Connect with Tasha Baron Smith

Website: www.tashabaronsmith.com

Facebook: https://www.facebook.com/tbaronsmith/

IG: @tashabaronsmith

BRENDA BURTON decided to obey God and leave her birthplace in California, and now resides in Houston, TX. That's when she began her journey, and what was always inside of her was able to be born and live.

Connect with Brenda:

Linkedin: Brenda Burton Ministries

Facebook: Making a Positive Change

Website: www.brendaburtonministry.com

CHRYSTAL CASTILLO is a wife, mother of two, Literary Engineer and CEO of ANN IT SO, a professional writing service that empowers business owners and non-profit organizations by helping them craft their vision and amplify their impact through compelling writing. She is also the Author of Affirmed, a Do-votional for Women.

Connect with Chrystal Castillo

Instagram: @ann.itisso

SHAKEIMA CLARK CHATMAN, a Charleston, SC native, is a dedicated real estate consultant and owner of The Chatman Group, where her mission is to make the American Dream accessible to all. She leverages her experience in education, corporate training, and software consulting to deliver exceptional service to her clients. Shakeima is the founder of D.I.V.A.S In

Training, a nonprofit organization empowering teenage girls to strive for success and honor. A recognized REALTOR® of Distinction, she holds the Accredited Buyer Representative Designation and Military Relocation Professional Certification. Shakeima is also the author of *Possess the Land: The Believer's Guide to Home Buying.*

Connect with Shakeima

Facebook: Shakeima Chatman

Instagram: @coachkeima

LinkedIn: chatmangroupsc

ANIKA DAVIS is a skilled professional with over two decades of experience in Human Services and is known for her sincere desire to assist and support individuals in achieving their goals. Anika is the Founder of Steppn Out, LLC, a coaching and consulting company that encourages and empowers youth and women to step out on faith and step into their next. Her passion for helping others led her to author Meditations of a Mother's

Heart, a book that uses poetry to inspire and encourage women of all ages.

Connect with Anika Davis

Instagram: @iamanikadavis

Website: www.steppinoutcc.com

DR. ANGELA CRUTCHFIELD, a seasoned entrepreneur and leadership consultant, blends her diverse experiences in business and ministry to offer transformative insights. With a deep commitment to prayer and spirituality, she brings a unique perspective to the intersection of faith and business. With a wealth of experience as a certified coach and public speaker, Dr. Angela inspires entrepreneurs to embrace prayer as a powerful tool for navigating business challenges. Through her leadership consultancy and lifestyle coaching, she equips entrepreneurs with prayer principles to cultivate resilience, vision, and divine guidance in their entrepreneurial endeavors.

Connect with Dr. Angela Crutchfield

Instagram: @wholenesslifestylecoach

Facebook: Wholeness Lifestyle Coach, Dr. Angela Crutchfield

YouTube: @wholenesslifestyle

LinkedIn: Dr. Angela Crutchfield

TikTok: @wholenesslifestylecoach

X: Wholeness_Coach

Websites: www.drangelacrutchfield.com,

www.crutchfieldgroupllc.com

KAYSIAN GORDON is a mother, financial advisor, author, writer, speaker, and Bible teacher. Kaysian is a full-time financial advisor and continues to share the messages of hope and love that God lays on her heart. She has successfully combined faith in the financial planning process with her clients.

Connect with Kaysian

Facebook: Kaysian Gordon

Instagram: KaysiGordon

LinkedIn: Kaysian Gordon

Website: www.kaysigordon.com

DR. PATRICE MAY is known to inspire as the host of the Be InSpire Lifestyle Show, a platform where she inspires others to tap into their God-given creativity. She is a Kingdom builder who is dedicated to prayer, a business owner, author, and conference speaker.

Connect with Dr. Patrice May

Instagram: @tricemay

Facebook: Patrice May

TikTok: @patricemay6925

YouTube: @The Be InSpired Lifestyle Show

STEPHANIE MONTGOMERY has been a New York Attorney for 24 years, a Real Estate Broker, and an Environmental Claims Adjuster for over 16 years. After many years of living my life for others and not feeling fulfilled, I heard God's voice whisper the game plan and strategy for an international women's empowerment organization that I founded called SestraNow (Sestra means Sister and NOW stands for  Network of Women). Finally, I have found my true God-given purpose in passionately pursuing SestraNow's mission to empower all women mentally, physically, and financially.

Connect with Stephanie Montgomery

Instagram: @sestranow

LinkedIn: SestraNow, LLC and SestraNow Consulting

Facebook: SestraNow International, SestraNow LLC,

   The Women Owned
   Business Network (Powered by SestraNow) and The
   Sisterhood Television Channel

Website: www.sestranow.com | www.setranowconsulting.com

NATASHA RICHARDS empowers mothers to thrive in life and business, she is also a passionate Mpowerment Coach and Author dedicated to guiding others toward personal and entrepreneurial success. With a heart for transformation and a commitment to nurturing growth, I inspire individuals to embrace their inner strength and overcome obstacles with faith and resilience.

Connect with Natasha Richards

Instagram: @Natasha.Richards.Coach

Website: www.MpoweredMe.com

LEWINFRED SHACK, MDiv is an ordained minister, author and licensed massage therapist with over 20 years' experience as a full-time entrepreneur. Shack embodies a lifestyle of wellness and shares the messages of resilience and hope at every opportunity.

Connect with LeWinfred Shack

Instagram: @TouchTheray901

Website: www.TouchTherapyLLC.com

ATHENA C. SHACK, MDiv, is the CEO of Watersprings Publisher and author of multiple books, the scripture writing/prayer journal series, Write. Listen. Pray.™ and designer of inspirational stationery. She is an ordained minister of the gospel and international speaker with a passion for the brokenhearted who teaches and proclaims God's power of redemption and  restoration. As a business owner, she has a mission to deliver books and resources to the marketplace that refresh the spirit, renew the mind, and restore the soul. Her debut book, *Grace for the Journey,* also bears the name of her ministry that empowers believers to overcome life's challenges with the grace of God in route to their destiny. At the end of the day, she's a busy mom of an artsy young lady and two charming boys, and wife to her amazing husband.

Connect with Athena C. Shack

Instagram: @thepublishingboss, @Write.Listen.Pray,

@waterspringspublishing

Facebook: Athena C. Shack, The Publishing Boss

Websites: www.thepublishingboss.com,

www.waterspringspublishing.com,

www.writelistenpray.com

STACY Y. THOMAS, MDiv, is an Author, Speaker, and Beauty Entrepreneur who is passionate about seeing people whole and living their best lives. She is the host of Cultivating Conversations, a podcast that tackles tough topics with the intent of fostering healthy conversations and cultivating hearts. She is also the proud mom of two beautiful young ladies.

Connect with Stacy Y. Thomas

Instagram: @iamstacy.t, @idesignbeautyllc

Websites: www.iamstacyt.com | www.idesignbeauty.com

LATOYIA BYRD-WILLIAMS is an accomplished consultant, leader, author and book editor with extensive experience driving strategic growth and fostering high-performing teams. As a member of an executive team, she has excelled in providing visionary leadership and managing critical organizational processes, including recruitment, onboarding, performance management, and DEI initiatives. She is the CEO of On Purpose Services, LLC., a consultant company.

Connect with Latoyia Byrd-Williams

Website: www.onpurposeservicesllc.com

REV. JOY W. YANCY, Authorpreneur and Pastor, encourages her readers to always be joyful. Pastor Joy stands on the premise "the joy of the Lord is her strength" (Nehemiah 8:10) and she inspires her social media audience to do the same with her daily "Morning Joy" posts.

Connect with Rev. Joy W. Yancy

Instagram: @morning_joy08

Facebook: Morning Joy with Pastor Joy

Website: www.joywyancy.com

www.ingramcontent.com/pod-product-compliance
Lightning Source LLC
Chambersburg PA
CBHW061747050726
47598CB00002B/616